What This Book Will Do for You

After reading this book, you will be able to create a résumé that effectively and attractively presents your experience and abilities. You will also know how to tailor your résumé to the needs of a prospective employer and how to use it to gain an interview—the all-important first hurdle in finding the best job for you. So read on . . .

Other Titles in the Successful Office Skills Series

HOW TO
Write
An Effective
Résumé

BOBBI LINKEMER

amacom
AMERICAN MANAGEMENT ASSOCIATION

This book is available at a special
discount when ordered in bulk quantities.
For information, contact Special Sales Department,
AMACOM, a division of
American Management Association,
135 West 50th Street, New York, NY 10020.

Library of Congress Cataloging-in-Publication Data

Linkemer, Bobbi.
     How to write an effective resume.

     (The Successful office skills series)
     Includes index.
     1. Résumés (Employment)   I. Title.   II. Series.
HF5383.L56   1987   650.1'4   86-47813
ISBN 0-8144-7669-4 (pbk.)

Printing number

10 9 8 7 6 5 4

CONTENTS

Introduction
Why You Need a Résumé

Here's a fact that may surprise you. If you're a young person in the first 5 years of your career, the chances are excellent that during the next 40 to 50 years, you will have at least five or six different careers—not only different jobs but jobs in *totally diverse fields.*

So unless you are one of that vanishing breed who joins a firm right out of school, works his or her way up through the ranks from mail clerk to CEO, and retires with the proverbial gold watch, you can pretty well count on changing jobs several times before your working life comes to an end.

Changes in careers or jobs can be traumatic and unsettling. With each such change, you are introducing yourself to new people, selling yourself and your skills to new buyers, creating an impression of you and what you can bring to a new organization. And often your entire sales pitch is contained on a single piece of paper that must say it all for you—your résumé. If your résumé doesn't get you in the door for that all-important first interview, you may never even get the chance to introduce or sell yourself in person.

Karen Kincaid didn't even have a résumé when her first potential job change practically fell into her lap. After less than a year of college, Karen had decided to try the working world for a while, just until she focused on her real interests and decided what to major in, she told herself. That was 11 years ago, and she was still with the same company—ACME Corporation.

She'd had her share of promotions. She had come to ACME as a clerk-typist at the age of 19. Now, at 30, she was the supervisor of an entire group of typists and administrative assistants. Not bad for a college dropout, she thought. At least that's what she thought most of the time, when she wasn't having trouble making ends meet on her salary.

Karen knew she had accumulated a lot of valuable experience in 11 years and that she probably had a lot to offer another employer. She knew, too, from talking to others in the company, that she was bumping her head against an invisible ceiling at ACME. No matter how many promotions or raises she got, she would never have the one thing she really wanted—to break out of the "administrative" mold and be considered part of the "professional" staff. At ACME, the gap between those two categories was simply too wide to cross.

Sometimes that really bothered her, and she would think about writing a résumé and sending it some-where—just to see what was out there. It was during one of her "bothered times" that the phone call came, and the idea of a résumé became an immediate need rather than just a vague thought. The phone call was from her friend Ellen, who worked in personnel at Federated Finance Company.

Federated was looking for an office manager, Ellen told her. She had the want ad right in front of her, ready to call the newspaper and place it in the Sunday edition. "This job has your name all over it," Ellen insisted. "I know the vice-president who's trying to fill this job, and I can give you a recommendation. All you have to do is send me a résumé, and I'll pass it along to him."

It sounded too good to be true, as Ellen described the job. Every one of the requirements matched some aspect of Karen's experience with ACME. The job did seem to have her name on it. Yet she wasn't nearly as excited as Ellen had expected her to be. "What's the matter with you?" Ellen finally asked. "I don't have a résumé," Karen told her. "Oh, is *that* all?" Ellen re-sponded impatiently, as if that had not been worth mentioning. "Just throw one together, and get it to me by sometime next week. It shouldn't be all that compli-cated."

Karen stared at the phone for a long time. Maybe it shouldn't be "all that complicated" to write a résumé, she thought; but somehow, she sensed that it would be for her. She didn't have the slightest idea how or where to begin. Perhaps she should just forget the whole thing. She could never do it by next week, anyway. That just wasn't possible!

But the job had sounded so perfect, it was hard to just forget it. Karen knew she could do that job. All she had to do was meet that vice-president and convince him that she could to it. And to meet him, she would need a résumé—by next week.

Karen's story is not unusual. Opportunities, with *your* name on them, are all around you, like doors waiting to be opened. One of the keys to opening those doors is an effective, targeted résumé. Do you need one? Absolutely. "Almost everyone needs a résumé!" insists a human resources professional whose business is reading them by the hundreds every week. "Unless your name is a household word, and your achievements are legendary, *you need a résumé*."

Do you have one? If you got a phone call like the one Karen received, or if you saw an ad for the perfect job, do you think the résumé you have is effective enough to do its job? And do you know what that job is?

If your answer to any of those questions is no or even a qualified maybe, this book will change your response to a confident *YES*.

Chapter 1

Selling You— You Gotta Know the Territory

Let's start this chapter by clearing up a few common misconceptions and answering some of the most important questions about résumés. If you know what they're really supposed to accomplish and what they were never intended to do at all, writing one may not seem such an awesome task.

What Is a Résumé?

One book on résumé preparation describes it as "a toothpaste commercial," explaining that the average employment manager devotes about the same amount of time to scanning a résumé that most television viewers spend watching a commercial designed to sell toothpaste—about 30 seconds. But rather than advertising the features and benefits of toothpaste, a résumé is designed to advertise the accomplishments and track record of its author—you.

Think for a moment about the concept of marketing. Marketing means taking a careful look at the needs of a certain segment of consumers and finding a way to satisfy those needs. A résumé is, fundamentally, a marketing tool. The consumer is the employment manager or the person in the company who makes the hiring decisions. The needs of that consumer are the requirements of the position he or she is trying to fill. You are the product, and your qualifications for that job are the way in which you will meet that employer's needs. And your first form of advertising will be your résumé.

As with any kind of marketing, it will require some digging to discover or uncover what the consumer really wants. Before Karen could begin to write her résumé, she thought she should have a better handle on Federated Finance's job requirements. She was right. When she called her friend Ellen back to ask her to reread the ad for Sunday's paper, Karen was on her way to doing her own market research. We'll talk about how you can do yours in a later chapter. For now, it's enough to remember that knowing the needs of your "market" is a vital step in getting ready to write an effective résumé.

What *Isn't* a Résumé?

Another way to understand what a résumé should be is to look at what it shouldn't be. Obviously, if it is a marketing tool, it is not a chronicling of everything you've ever done or experienced with no regard for how that list meets an employer's needs.

A résumé, then, is not your entire life story, because your entire life could not possibly be relevant to the requirements of a single job. It is not cutesy or amateurish or contrived. If you want anyone to read it, it is obviously not a cluttered, wordy, unreadable mess. And most important, it is never a work of fiction, full of exaggerations, inaccuracies, or just pure fabrications.

What Is a Résumé
Supposed to Accomplish?

Karen would be wrong if she assumed that her résumé had to convince Federated's vice-president that she could fill the office manager position. That is not its purpose at all. What her résumé *should* accomplish is to create an image of Karen Kincaid in the vice-president's mind. According to Patricia Mathews, a human resources manager for a *Fortune* 500 company in the Midwest: "A résumé creates an image first. If that image is a positive one, it will lead to an interview. That's all it does. That's all it's supposed to do."

Everyone who has ever been through an interview that did not lead to a job offer knows very well that those are two distinctly separate issues. Pat Mathews likes to compare a résumé to a product brochure. "I may love the brochure describing a Toyota Corolla," she says. "That brochure may even lure me to the showroom. But I have never bought a car based solely on a product brochure, and I don't know of anyone who has."

Who Needs a Résumé?

Some employment counselors say *everyone* needs one. Like Karen, you never know when the phone will ring or opportunity will knock, and you will be sorry you didn't start this project sooner. However, a résumé should be tailored to the requirements of the position for which you're applying. If you subscribe to the concept of a résumé as a marketing tool, that advice makes a lot of sense.

"The style of the résumé, to a degree, must be related to the style and expectations of the person receiving it," advises Elbert W. Burr, a private consultant on careers and organizational change. Burr, who recalls scanning 32,000 résumés in a single year, not only advocates targeting your résumé but feels you should have more than one. "I never talk to people about a single résumé," he says. "I always talk about having several. You have to ask yourself, 'What accomplishments are most significant to the receiver?' If you have more than one receiver, you'll need more than one résumé."

If a résumé should, as Burr suggests, reflect the style of the person receiving it, surely it should also reflect the style of the person sending it. People in different stages of their lives and careers do have different styles, as well as different levels of experience and different job goals. If a résumé is your personal advertisement, one of the things it must do is express your unique style and message.

The job changer who seeks professional growth, like Karen Kincaid; the person who is bored or unfulfilled and decides to risk seeking a new career; someone who has just been laid off or fired and must start over, just when his or her confidence is at its lowest point; and even the longtime worker who decides to resume his or her education and begins to seek the right graduate program in the right school—these are all people who will need to develop a résumé that will do its job. By now, you know that that job is to create an image—a first impression of the writer—that will lead to an interview. That's the résumé's job; yours is to do the rest.

Chapter 2

Let's Get This Show on the Road

Where Do You Start?

Getting started when you don't know where or how to begin is a bit like facing a mountain and wondering how you'll ever get to the top. This is exactly how Karen Kincaid viewed her promise to get a résumé to Ellen by next week. Even with a copy of Sunday's ad describing the job and a book from the library on résumé writing, she wasn't at all certain what to do first.

She decided to begin by thinking about what she had to offer. Karen's reasoning was right on the mark. If a résumé is, as Pat Mathews suggests, "a product brochure," the person writing it had better know the product pretty well. That may sound ridiculous, considering that you will be writing about yourself, and, obviously, you know yourself very well after all these years. Or do you?

It's not as easy as it sounds to write about yourself. Try it. Pick up a pad of paper and a pen or sit down at a typewriter and write a paragraph about you. Pretend for a moment that you are trying to describe yourself to someone you've never met, someone you'd like to impress so that he or she will *want* to meet you. Include anything you think will influence this person—all the positive things you can think of, all your best qualities, everything impressive about you.

If you're like most people, you may have had a bit of difficulty with that paragraph—not because you really don't know yourself or are unable to string words into coherent sentences but because you didn't know exactly what to include and what to leave out. After spending an entire lifetime with yourself, you have accumulated a virtual library of data about your favorite subject. When it's time to select only a little bit of that data to put in a single paragraph, how do you know what's important and appropriate and what's totally irrelevant?

There are two challenges involved in doing this little exercise and in writing your résumé: (1) You have to collect as much information about yourself and your attributes and achievements as you can possibly discover, uncover, or remember; and (2) you must reorganize that information so that it conveys a single, unified message to the reader.

Taking Inventory

Here is where the work begins; but before you shudder at that prospect, try thinking of this as a treasure hunt instead of an attic-cleaning project. Every piece of information you find and add to the pile is a gem of sorts, something you may never have thought of as important or valuable but that may well turn out to be just that.

Judy Dubin, president of Career Dimensions and a person who has helped hundreds of job seekers create résumés, advises: "Start with an attitude of curiosity, inquiry. Think of yourself as an explorer or a researcher. You must look internally. If you don't know the product," says Dubin, "you can't write the brochure."

O.K., you're settled down and ready to go. You've blocked out some time and found a quiet place to work. You've assumed an attitude of adventure and discovery rather than one of drudgery and pain, and you've assembled your favorite writing materials. Now what? Now you're going to make some lists. If you're using paper and pen, write your headings at the top of each page. If you're working on a computer or word processor, you'll just enter a list of file names, one for each heading.

The headings should include *Education, Positions*

Held, Areas of Expertise, Extracurricular or Not-for-Pay Activities, Things I Love to Do, Pipe Dreams, and any other categories you can think of that I've omitted. If all those topics seem awesome, they really aren't, especially when you take them one at a time.

What Have You Learned?

Let's start with *Education.* Since this one is the easiest for most people, it will help you flex your mental muscles and build some confidence. Write down all of the schools you've attended, beginning with the most recent and listing them in reverse chronological order. Along with the names of the schools, record the dates you attended; the city and state in which each was located; the degrees, diplomas, or certificates you received or expect to receive; and your major and minor subject areas in each school. Jot down your cumulative grade point average, honors and special commendations, and entrance exam or other test scores that seem impressive or noteworthy.

Next, think about any training you've had that was not part of an organized curriculum, such as seminars, correspondence courses, or any similar activities that enhanced your knowledge or competency in a certain area. Maybe you took a ten-session course on effective public speaking or signed up for a class in writing for fun and money at your community night school. Your company may have sent you to a seminar on basic selling techniques or learning to love your computer or people-handling skills for new managers. Perhaps you took art or piano or photography lessons on weekends, strictly for your own enjoyment. Write it all down. Go back as far as you can. Everything counts, even if you did it when you were ten.

This is an exercise in brainstorming, and when you brainstorm, *you don't edit.* You don't say, "Well, I did take that Saturday class in ceramics; but that has absolutely nothing to do with my career, so it probably doesn't count." It counts. *Everything* counts. When you brainstorm, every idea has equal value. Judy Dubin suggests you try one simple rule as you make your lists: Suspend value judgments! "Imagine that everything counts equally. Nothing matters more or less than anything else; and if everything is equally important, you'll be able to see the patterns in what you've written."

But looking for patterns comes later in the process. For now, it's important to remember that if something fits the criteria, it goes on the list, no matter how irrelevant it may seem at first.

Where Have You Worked?

If you've exhausted your store of educational or learning experiences for now, go on to the next list—*Positions Held.* On this one, you'll list all the jobs you've had for which you were paid. Again, start with your present or most recent position, and list the rest so that the last one on the list is the first job you ever held.

With each listing, include: the full name of the company, spelled and punctuated correctly (if you don't know, you can look it up later); your title or, if you didn't have one, a "made-up" title that accurately describes what you did; the city and state where the company is located; and the beginning and ending dates of your employment (month and year will do). There's much more to do with this list, but since your purpose here is to at least *begin* all the lists in one sitting, if possible, you can come back to this one later.

What Do You Do Well?

Now you're ready to toot your own horn a bit. Under *Areas of Expertise,* you're going to write down everything you do well or know a lot about. When Karen Kincaid did her list, for example, she included:

1. Speedy and accurate typing
2. Psychological test scoring
3. Intimate knowledge of most business office equipment

These were all things that she didn't want to do again but that she realized were definitely among her strong suits. Sifting through some of the skills she did want to cultivate, she also wrote:

4. Motivating people
5. Organizing and managing systems
6. Juggling 15 tasks at once without losing my cool

This is one of the harder lists to write, for a number of reasons. Most people are reluctant or just plain unable to toot their own horns, and you may be one of those who feels awkward doing it. Also, you may not be used to thinking in terms of what you do very well or how you qualify as a miniexpert. But if someone asked you to list all the things you *don't* do very well or all the subjects about which you feel you know absolutely nothing, you could probably fill pages. Well, just apply the same techniques, only in a positive direction.

You'll achieve two things: a solid list of real skills and strengths, and a new and infinitely more satisfying way of looking at yourself. Even if this list weren't important for your résumé, it would be a good use of your time and energy.

"But," cautions Judy Dubin, "brainstorming is hard to do in your head or alone. Most people don't think they have anything to offer—even talented people. That's why it's helpful to do this with a friend and have that person respond to what you're saying." We'll talk more about using your friends as sounding boards in the next chapter.

What Have You Contributed to the World?

On the *Extracurricular Activities* page, you will write down everything you can think of that you've ever done as a volunteer, just as you did with jobs for which you were paid. This is another archeological expedition, requiring a lot of careful digging into your past. As you dig, you may wonder whether you should write down such things as:

- Organized and peformed in a magic show in my garage to raise money for the Jerry Lewis Telethon.
- Campaigned for a political candidate in my township.
- Worked as a volunteer for our community center's blood drive.

You certainly should. They were all things you did that counted but for which you were not paid. They tell a lot about you, not the least of which is that you have an awareness of, and interest in, civic activities, demonstrate a consistent concern for people, and are a team player. That's just one of the patterns you will begin to discover when you study these lists with a fresh perspective.

What Do You Enjoy Doing?

By now, this should be getting a little easier and maybe more like a game and less like a chore. Certainly, making a list of *Things I Love to Do* shouldn't be too painful. Things you love to do should also include things at which you've achieved some measure of success. Karen played the guitar and sang, and those were both activities she enjoyed. She put them on her list. You might include special achievements in school—all the way back to high school or beyond—like being a cheerleader or a member of the debating team, teaching Sunday school because you genuinely enjoyed kids, or working on your school newspaper or your organization's publicity committee. The list is as individual as you are and as long as your interests.

What Do You Dream of Doing?

Pipe Dreams is the place where you can really let your imagination run wild. It's another way of saying, These are things I'd like to do or jobs I'd like to have or ways in which I'd like to spend most of my waking hours. Before you begin to write anything down, close your eyes for a few minutes and fantasize. How *would* you like to spend your days? If you could do any kind of work in the world, what would it be? Don't be reasonable or rational. Remember the first rule of brainstorming: Don't edit! That's why this section is called *Pipe Dreams*.

If you want to be a newspaper reporter or a novelist but have never had a class in writing, put it down anyway. If you'd like to run a small company of your own someday but have no money in the bank and can't even read a financial statement, so what? If you dream of climbing mountains and shooting the rapids but feel that's hardly a "career," forget what you think of as *the rules* and put it on the list. Get the idea? O.K., go to it.

By this time, you're either (*A*) exhausted or (*B*) exhilarated. If *A* is the case, walk away from the lists for now. If *B* is true, go back to *Positions Held* for one more trip down memory lane.

What Have You Accomplished?

Look back at the list of jobs you've held or things you've done for which you earned money. This is the place where people usually show the "responsibilities" that went with each position or provide some other form of job description, which tells the potential employer all about expectations but little about achievements.

You're going to try Judy Dubin's approach instead. She calls it PAR, which stands for *p*roblems-*a*ctions-*r*esults. Look at each job on the list and ask yourself: What problems did I encounter when I did this job? What actions did I take to solve them? And what were the results of those actions?

There are probably 15 different ways to describe a job, but this one has a few obvious advantages. First, it's a fairly straightforward method of uncovering the information you will need later. Second, it's a practical way to organize that information. Third, it emphasizes action and accomplishments, not responsibilities. The accompanying sidebar shows an example of how Karen used PAR to describe only one of the problems she had dealt with in her present job.

Example: The PAR Approach

Position Held: Supervisor, Administrative Staff, ACME Corporation, Bloomfield, Conn.

Problem 1: Attic storage for supplies and other materials in complete disarray; no inventory system; improper storage; poor lighting, limited space; need to prepare for future storage requirements.

Actions:

1. Developed inventory forms; set up formal inventory system.
2. Ordered shelving for additional storage space.
3. Drew floor plan of attic to locate materials at a glance.
4. Discarded old, out-of-date materials.
5. Organized and rearranged all stored materials.

Results:

1. Quantity of anything stored in the attic can now be determined at any time.
2. It is now easy for any employee to find materials in the attic.
3. Monthly inventory reports create accurate inventory projections.
4. The attic is no longer a fire hazard due to improper storage.
5. Improved use of space freed up additional room in the attic for present and future storage.

Congratulations! You've completed the toughest part of the process. Your lists are finished—well, almost finished—and the rest is downhill. Why *almost* finished? Because brainstorming is not really a solitary activity. Now that you've done the spadework, it's time to call in a friend—or a professional—and begin to use those building blocks to construct a résumé.

Chapter 3

Decisions, Decisions, Decisions

Choosing a Partner

You've just spent a great deal of time and energy on the first phase of your "treasure hunt"—composing your lists. It may feel as if you're finished and ready to get down to the business of putting it all in some finished form, but you're not. No, it's not an endless project, but it does involve more than making lists.

For one thing, you know by now that brainstorming by yourself is not an easy task. You haven't had any feedback on what you've written. You haven't heard any suggestions or the kind of questions that would help you dig even deeper. You need another person to use as a sounding board, among other things.

Here's where the choices begin. Who should that other person be—a friend, a relative, a total stranger? Do you know someone who can look at what you've done and what remains to be done dispassionately and objectively? Do you have a friend who thinks creatively, who looks at things in an entirely different way than you do?

Karen was fortunate. She had a friend, David, in another department at ACME, who always seemed to come at problems from a different direction than she did. He was someone Karen both trusted and respected—in short, the perfect choice for a brainstorming partner.

Feeling like someone cramming for an exam, Karen had spent half the night compiling her lists. The next day, she took them to David and asked for his help. During lunch, they pored over the lists, while David threw out ideas and questions.

Finally, he said: "I can see a couple of threads running through all of these lists. One is great organizational and problem-solving ability. It looks as if you've had to bring order out of chaos in most of the jobs you've held and in your volunteer work. I get the impression that you really get excited when you've got a big problem to tackle." He was right, and Karen was surprised that she hadn't picked up that thread herself.

"I can also see that a lot of the things you've done and seem to enjoy doing involve people," David continued. "It seems to me that you're a real people motivator. For someone who wants to be a manager, that's a pretty important element."

By the time the lunch hour ended, Karen had another list—this one labeled *Patterns*. It was a page of observations David had made as he studied what she had already written and what they had both added to her inventory.

Using Professionals

David was someone who saw patterns that tied seemingly unrelated entries on different lists into one clear message. If you've searched your mind and can't come up with a soul who thinks like David, you might consider going to a professional career counselor or résumé service. What you'd be looking for is *not* someone to write your résumé for you but someone who will ask you the right questions and see the broad pictures you may have missed.

Career advisers, like Judy Dubin, who runs her own firm, and Pat Mathews, who provides the same service within a large corporation, are not the same as résumé services. In fact, they never write someone else's résumé. "It's not authentic if I write it," insists Dubin. "It must be in their own words, not mine. My role is to work with clients to help them generate and organize data. I'd rather see people read a good book and write their own résumé than go to a service."

The general feeling among many counselors and employment managers is that résumé services may be helpful when you're making a dramatic career change but often create résumés that are almost interchangeable in their sameness. If your résumé is to be a marketing tool to fit your unique qualifications to an employer's equally unique job requirements, it will have to be one of a kind.

Technical Capabilities

Stop for a few minutes and assess your strengths in two areas: How well do you communicate your ideas in writing? And how would you assess your design capabilities? We're not looking for a Hemingway here. The idea is to be able to write in a direct, uncluttered style, to spot and correct inconsistencies in grammar and structure, and to organize your thoughts coherently.

Are you nodding in agreement as you read that description, or are you shaking your head and thinking, "I can't string two sentences together and have them make any sense"? If you really have no confidence in your ability to write clearly, you may want to get help—either on the front end, before you write a single word, or after you've done a rough draft and feel the need for some editing.

Now how good is your graphic sense? Can you organize elements on a page so that they don't force the reader to look everywhere at once, not knowing where to focus attention? When you look at a page of type, can you tell if it's balanced or heavy on one side, cluttered or comfortable to read, pleasing to the eye? Then, if you had to re-create that page, could you do a better job?

On the mechanical side, can you type accurately, or do you know someone who can? If you should decide to get your résumé typeset rather than typed, would you know how to choose a type style that met your needs? Are you familiar with duplicating or printing methods and what they can and can't do?

This brief inventory of your editorial and graphic skills should give you a rough idea of whether you can tackle the technical side of résumé preparation alone or whether you will need help. If you think you're going to need assistance, you have an array of options.

Sometimes friends are gold mines of expertise and knowledge you never dreamed they had. You may know someone with a background in English or journalism who would gladly give you a hand with punctuation and grammar. Or you may have an artistic friend who would be happy to help you set up your format, from simple arranging of paragraphs on the page to a full-scale design, if that's what you decide you want. Another option, of course, is to hire a professional in any of the areas you need or to bring the whole thing to a résumé service and ask for help in putting it together.

The important thing, when you do use a service, is to be sure you supply the basic information and that the words are yours, not those of the staff at the résumé service. The final product must reflect *you* and who you are. If the résumé is too slick or too common, it may not even be taken seriously by employment managers, who have become wary of documents they consider "manufactured."

"In fact," notes Marvin McMillian, Ph.D., and vice-president of human resources for a major utility company, "most personnel people have come to distrust résumés in general. The more sophisticated they are, the more skeptical I am." Dr. McMillian tends to discount most of the fancy résumés he sees because they all look alike. "People have become very artful," he observes, "at hiding gaps and claiming skills they don't have."

Some résumés are guilty of either or both of those sins. That's why it's important to select the type of résumé that will convey your message honestly and convincingly, without creating suspicion in the mind of the person reading it.

Types of Résumés

Different kinds of résumés are designed to achieve different objectives. They accomplish their goals by organizing information in different ways.

The *chronological* résumé is the most traditional form, the one most employers are used to seeing. It lists everything in reverse chronological order, from the most recent back to the earliest, just as you did on your *Positions Held* and *Education* lists. In fact, if you decide to use this format, you've already done much of the necessary preparation. Because employers are familiar with it, they often prefer it to other types.

On the plus side, the chronological résumé is orderly and easy to read and interpret. Employers can see at a glance what you've done, what positions you've held, how your career has progressed, and the consistency or diversity of your jobs and activities. If you've been marching steadily ahead, from job to better job in the same field, a chronological résumé makes your career path as clear as the yellow brick road.

If, on the other hand, your career path looks more like one cut through jungle underbrush than a clearly discernible road, you may not want to use this format. A chronological résumé shines a spotlight on gaps and inconsistencies in your work life but not necessarily on your special skills and strengths.

The *functional* résumé highlights areas of similarity or consistency. When your pattern of progress in a specific career is sketchy at best, but when you've had some convincing success experience in two or three broad categories, a functional résumé will deliver that message. It will also help potential employers draw the conclusions you want them to draw.

And that's exactly what many employers don't like about the functional résumé. "I want to make these judgments for myself," says Dr. McMillian. "If you're applying for a marketing job, I want to see that you've held some positions that show me you could do this job. If you're just getting out of school, I want to look at your activities, the courses you've taken—particularly marketing courses."

As a former personnel administrator, Ramona Howard, now vice-president of Drake Beam Morin, a human resources consulting firm, tends to agree with that point of view. "I advise people to do a functional résumé if they have gaps or if they're targeting a particular field where they have some experience to offer," says Howard, "but I also encourage my clients to go with whatever feels most comfortable to them. Accomplishments can be handled effectively in either form, and every résumé I'm involved with *has to include accomplishments*."

The *combination* résumé is actually a blend of the best of both the above formats. It lists in chronological order the entries under each heading you decide to include, but it also has a section that focuses on areas of strength or competence. Since it's a hybrid, it shares most of the advantages and few of the disadvantages of the two styles it combines. If it's well constructed, it can be very effective. If it's not, it may look like a hodgepodge that couldn't decide which way to go.

Elbert W. Burr, an outplacement specialist who has spent much of his long career helping fired or laid-off executives reposition themselves in the work world, recommends his own version of the combination résumé. Acknowledging that a chronology of experience is "essential, though overrated," Burr likes to hide it on the second page, especially if there have been a number of job changes. On the first page, he stresses three essential elements: (1) an objective, (2) a summary of qualifications, and (3) a list of accomplishments to support those qualifications.

The *promotional* résumé is truly a one-of-a-kind creation, flaunting all the rules and often being more than a little brash and flashy. Its purpose is to sell you and your experience in an unconventional manner, and its form may be as varied and unique as its subject. It may, for example, be a well-designed letter that tells it all and takes the place of a résumé. It may be in narrative form or reflect the industry to which it's targeted.

If it's well thought-out and designed, it can be as effective as a rifle shot aimed directly at its target. If it misses the mark, though, it runs the risk of coming across as contrived, cutesy, overdone, and unprofessional. A person seeking a job in the restaurant industry whose vital information is presented on a menu has created a cliché. A journalist who uses dramatic headlines and a news story about himself or herself is walking a very fine line. Promotional résumés have to be used with care, be carefully targeted, and, above all, be tasteful.

How Do You Choose?

For someone like Karen, who had worked for only one company during her entire career but had held a series of positions within that company, at least three of the four styles would have been appropriate. She had no trouble eliminating the promotional résumé from her possible choices, but each of the others had its own appeal. She finally chose the combination approach, listing her job titles and basic responsibilities in reverse order on page 2 and concentrating her major efforts on writing a job objective based on Federated's ad in the Sunday paper, a summary of her qualifications for that specific job, and a list of her accomplishments at ACME.

To determine which style is best suited to your needs, ask yourself the following questions, and see how the advice fits your answers:

1. *Does my experience flow logically from one job to another, or does it zigzag all over the place, revealing gaps and inconsistencies?* If it flows logically, you could certainly use a chronological résumé; if it's a patchwork quilt of colorful but unrelated pieces, assess your strong points and go with the functional style.
2. *If it does map out a clearly defined career path in one field, do I want to remain in that field, or would I rather do something entirely different?* If you want to keep growing in the field in which

you're now working, the chronological résumé will underscore your progress. If, on the other hand, you want to change careers, a functional résumé might be more effective in building a bridge between the two paths.

3. *If I do want to change directions, have I identified areas of strength that would be appropriate to where I want to go?* If you haven't, go back to your lists and do some more prospecting. You didn't decide to change directions based on nothing. The basis for your decision must be running through at least some of those lists, especially the one headed *Things I Love to Do.*

4. *Am I targeting a very specific line of work for which I am so uniquely qualified that my résumé must be tailored to that job and only that job?* Here is a made-to-order opportunity to try a promotional résumé; but remember, it's either going to be very effective or a total bomb. There's no gray area on this one.

5. *Do I know what I want, or am I trying to hit a moving target blindfolded?* Maybe this question should have come first, because it's definitely the toughest to answer. If you don't know what you want, don't start writing your résumé!

Go back to your lists one more time. Start with *Pipe Dreams.* After all, that is where you wrote all the things you would do to earn a living if this were the best of all possible worlds and you could do anything you wanted to do. Up till now, I've said you don't edit when you brainstorm. This is the time to edit.

Unless what you've written is truly impossible—like wanting to be a brain surgeon when you've never gotten a decent grade in science, dropped out of college, and just celebrated your fifty-seventh birthday—reexamine those dreams. Somewhere in them, there is a possible, maybe even probable, career choice.

Your other lists are equally fertile ground for unharvested ideas. Cross off only the absolutely crazy, totally impossible ones, and go back to your brainstorming partner to explore what's left. Then read on. The next chapter looks even more closely at how you should proceed when you have no idea what you want to do for a living.

Chapter 4

Wanted—
One Job Description
with Your Name on It

What Do You Want?

Karen Kincaid was lucky: She didn't have to struggle to discover what kind of a job she might like to have. When she heard about the position of office manager at Federated, she knew it really did "have her name on it." All she really had to do was tailor her résumé to those requirements.

Not everyone is that fortunate. Unless you are applying for a specific position you know you want and are qualified to do, as Karen did, you may be whistling in the wind when you send out your résumé. "Most people just write a résumé," observes Judy Dubin, the president of Career Dimensions. "They don't know what they want or even what's out there."

But new career options and opportunities are *everywhere.* You just have to know how to look, develop a new way of seeing what is not immediately apparent.

If you've gone back to your lists and poked around in *Things I Love to Do* and *Pipe Dreams,* you've probably already uncovered a few clues. Even one is enough to get you started on the next part of this treasure hunt.

Let's say you've uncovered a pattern you never saw before—an interest in writing. You once won an essay contest—in fourth grade, but you did win it. You worked on your high school newspaper and helped write the entertainment skit for your college fraternity or sorority. In your present job, a big part of your responsibilities includes writing reports and memos, and you always get compliments on their clarity and incisiveness. Of the things you do at work, you realize that writing those reports, which some of your colleagues dread, is an assignment you genuinely enjoy.

You may uncover other patterns as well; several are probably buried in the data you've already gathered. But let's just see where this one will lead us. There are two places to look when you're searching for the kind of work you want to do: One is inside yourself, which you did when you wrote and studied your lists; and the other is "out there" in the world. You've already spent a lot of time exploring your inner universe. Now let's talk about how you tackle the outer one.

What Is Out There?

It's a big world, even if you narrow that world down to the part of it that deals with business. How do you discover what kinds of work there are to do that might be a match for your interests and talents? You become an explorer and a researcher.

There are two places you're going to conduct your research. One is in the want-ad section of the newspaper; the other is more personal. If you've been job hunting for a while, you're probably already familiar with want ads. If you haven't been, now's a good time to start reading them.

Why would you go to the want ads if you're not actually looking for a job? One reason is that they are treasure maps leading you straight to jobs you may not have known existed or ever thought of as viable possibilities for you. The job itself isn't important. It's the broad *category of work* in which that job fits that matters right now.

The second reason is that you are now going to see where your interests—like an "interest in writing"— may lead you. What kinds of jobs require writing skills?

Do those jobs interest you? Do you know what else they encompass besides writing? Let's assume you've combed through several issues of the Sunday *New York Times* and the *National Business Employment Weekly,* as well as your local Sunday want-ad section. You've made a list of positions that include writing in their descriptions. On your list, you have such job titles as "assistant editor," "public relations associate," "manager–internal communications," "vice-president–public affairs," "technical writer," and "advertising copywriter."

Having read the ads, you have some idea of what each position involves; and you have become aware, even at this stage of your research, that writing jobs are as varied as species of birds. Now you want to do two things with the ads: First, try to get the feel of each job, based on what little you know; and second, find out more about the ones that interest you.

There's a trick to the first part. You have to turn off your head for a while, which means you are not going to ask yourself what you *think* about each of these jobs. Instead, you are going to tune in to how you *feel* about it. Close your eyes for a minute and imagine yourself doing that job. How does it feel? Wonderful? Exciting? Boring? Confining? Frightening? Just right? All wrong? If it feels right, it has potential for you; if it feels wrong, cross it off your list.

Asking the People Who Know

At this point, you've read the ads and discovered some writing jobs that interest you. You've tried to imagine yourself doing those jobs and eliminated the ones that seemed a poor fit. Now you're ready to find out more about the jobs you think you might like.

If you want to learn about different kinds of writing jobs and what it takes to do them, the best way is to talk to the people who work at those jobs every day. Finding the right people to talk to involves *networking*. Asking them to spend some time telling you about their work and how they feel about it is called *information interviewing*.

Where do you find these people? It only takes *one* to begin networking, and it only takes *one* who will talk to you to conduct an information interview. Take a mental inventory. Do you know a single person who writes as part or all of his or her job? Do you know anyone who might know a writer? Chances are the answer will be yes. If so, you're on your way. If not, go back to the ads. If there's a phone number or a company name, you can call. If it's a blind ad, you can write a letter.

What you want is an opportunity to talk to someone about each of these jobs or types of jobs. You want to know what the job involves, what kind of skills you would need to do it, what kind of background it takes to qualify, and where it might lead. You *don't* want to convey the idea that you're job hunting rather than information hunting. An information interview is just what it implies—a chance for you to gather information. You are not selling yourself here; you are doing research.

Once you find a single person to interview, you move into the networking part of the search. You have two objectives: to understand as much about different kinds of writing jobs as you can and to keep adding new people to your list to interview. Each time you talk to someone, ask that person if he or she knows anyone else you might call to request an interview. People in the writing field—or in any field—know their colleagues. Most will be happy to talk to you or to refer you to someone else who will talk to you. The rest is up to you.

You make the calls. You conduct the interviews. You follow up with thank-you notes. And you evaluate the information you gather. If you truly have a spirit of adventure, you will find this one of the most stimulating and rewarding endeavors of your life. You'll meet interesting, concerned people who will amaze you with their generosity; and you'll amass a mountain of valuable information about the kind of work you're investigating.

One word of caution: Longtime personnel executive Elbert W. Burr, who is an enthusiastic proponent of information interviewing, warns that not everyone feels as he does. You may call people who do not want to meet with you or share the names of their fellow professionals. Perhaps they don't have the time or the inclination to network. Says Burr: "There are a lot of very busy people. If someone declines, don't take it personally and don't get discouraged. Just go on to the next person."

What Do Employers Want?

If you have a want ad or a job description in your hands, or if you've been doing some information interviewing, by now you have a pretty good idea of what employers want (in your specific area of interest, at least). The other part of the question is, What will they be looking for *on your résumé?*

The answer depends on who you ask and where you look. One popular text on résumé preparation, for example, stresses the "qualities" employers seek and instructs readers on how to convey those qualities in their résumés. Qualities or characteristics are intangible and thus difficult to communicate. For one thing, it feels like bragging, which is not a trait that comes easily to most people. You may not know how to express such strengths as people-skills or writing ability or a sense of direction.

What you say and how you say it often convey those messages for you. If you've held a few positions in supervision and you've listed accomplishments that indicate how your management style has helped to motivate your staff, you've already told the reader something about your people-skills. If your résumé and cover letter are written in a clear, concise, readable manner, you've said volumes about your writing ability without ever mentioning it.

Let's go back to our experts for another perspective on what employers want to see. Dr. Marvin McMillian, vice-president of human resources for a large utility company, is looking for "relevant experience in the work world. Or if you're just out of college," says Dr. McMillian, "I want to see something in the college career that demonstrates your interest in this field—an internship, membership in an organization, activities."

He concentrates on the logical progression from one job to the next, the length of time you've held those jobs, and gaps in your work experience; and he doesn't agree with the textbook approach to conveying your strengths. "I don't pick up on strengths in a résumé," he says. "Unless I'm sure *you* wrote this résumé, there's nothing to indicate you wrote it or that you have good communication skills." How would he get any idea of what strengths you do have? "In the interview."

Pat Mathews, human resources manager for a *Fortune* 100 company in the Midwest, is equally emphatic. "Don't tell me you've got it, show me!" advises Mathews. "Show me you've got it by accomplishments." But she also reads between the lines of what you've written. "A job objective shows me you're a planner. A well-organized résumé shows me you're well organized."

Mathews adds a new dimension to what employment managers are seeking. "When someone in my position reads a résumé," she explains, "she is looking for a way *to screen you out.* I have to whittle that pile down."

Ramona Howard, vice-president of a human resources consulting firm, also screens out applicants—those who don't meet what she calls SKA: the basic *s*kills, *k*nowledge, and *a*bility to meet the job requirements. Sometimes, she says, she is "industry-specific," seeking a person with a publishing background to fill a position in the publishing industry. "But the personnel school of thought is to look for competence in a certain field and apply it to any industry."

Howard tries to get a feel for the previous work environment a résumé reveals. "Astute personnel administrators have some knowledge of corporate climates and management philosophies," she explains. "We know that someone coming from a collegial, participative environment might be aghast and lost in one that is more competitive and political."

By now you may be getting the impression that employment managers can see things you never intended them to see in your résumé. No, they don't have supernatural powers, but they certainly do have astute powers of observation.

Now that you have some idea of what employers want, you'll learn how to tell them you have it, what to include in your résumé, and what to leave out.

Chapter 5
It's Time to Toot Your Horn

How Do You Tell Them
You Have What They Want?

You know by now that you must have a handle on what the needs of the employer are and how you meet those needs. The needs of the employer comprise two elements: the requirements of the job and what that employment manager is looking for in your résumé to convince him or her you deserve an interview. Let's start with the requirements of the job. You will find them in a job description, so that's the first thing you'll need.

Where are you going to get a job description for this mythical job you're targeting? Well, first consider that it needn't be mythical. It can be a real job, advertised in the want-ad section of the paper, listed with the job-placement office at school, pinned on a bulletin board almost anywhere, obtained from the files of an employment agency, or mentioned to you by a friend or networking contact.

If that's the case, your task is going to be much like Karen's. You will read the job description, assess the appropriateness of your experience and qualifications, and select the right information to put in your résumé. If that's not the case, and you don't have a job description, or you aren't even aware of an exciting position that fits your desires, you will have to write one.

Writing a job description, at this point in the process, is hardly as difficult as it may have seemed a few chapters ago. You know a great deal more now than you did then—about what you're looking for and what it will take to do it; about what employers are looking for; and, most important, about yourself.

Putting Yourself in the Employer's Place

Step out of your own shoes for a moment and step into those of a potential employer. Imagine that you have a job to fill, and you're writing an ad. It's an entry-level position in your public relations department, reporting to the manager of external communications. You want someone with demonstrated writing ability, though not necessarily vast experience in the field. You're willing to work with this person and train him or her, because ability to understand and communicate the corporate message is a critical requirement for this job, as are the skills needed to influence newspaper editors to print your material. The job involves a lot of detail work, news-release writing, researching, poise under pressure, and sometimes, long hours.

Now pretend you are that manager of external communications, and write an ad for the job you're trying to fill. When you're finished, it might look something like what's shown in the accompanying sidebar.

Public Relations Assistant

Excellent entry-level opportunity for a writer in public relations department of major bank–holding company. Responsibilities include: writing news releases and other public relations-related copy; media relations and placement of newsworthy items; research; planning of special events; contributing articles to internal publications; and supervising photographers on assignment for the bank.

A qualified applicant must have at least a bachelor's degree, preferably in journalism or English; one to three years' experience in a position involving writing, dealing with the media, or special-event planning; ability to interact with a wide variety of people, juggle several tasks simultaneously, and work well under pressure.

Send résumé and salary requirements to P.O. Box 234, in care of this newspaper, Chicago, IL. 60606.

Why go through all of this? Because you cannot target your résumé to a vague idea; you can only target it to a set of real or assumed needs on the part of a potential employer. Let's take a quick look at the way Federated Finance described the position of office manager in its Sunday want ad, shown in a second sidebar.

Office Manager

Federated Finance Company is seeking an experienced Office Manager who is capable of working with administrative personnel to guide, support, and direct their efforts.

Responsibilities would include: hiring and terminating personnel; supervising administrative staff; maintaining and updating personnel files; processing work flow; establishing office procedures; conducting ongoing dialog with management and administration; providing input on equipment purchases and space planning; solving people and administrative problems; coordinating vacation and other leave time; and assuming responsibility for daily office management.

Candidate for the position should have at least five years' experience in management or supervision, familiarity with office policies and procedures, track record in developing and implementing office systems, and experience in working with all levels of management.

Whether you have a job description like Karen's or one you created yourself, you are now ready to look at the elements that compose a résumé.

What Do You Include?

This section will deal with how to organize your information. Let's begin with the basic headings one veteran résumé reader describes as the essentials: "Objective," "Qualifications," and "Accomplishments."

The objective. Pat Mathews often sees 200 to 300 résumés a day—or perhaps, "a night" would be more accurate. Her days are sometimes so full, she packs them into her briefcase and brings them home to read later. "Later" often turns out to be about 11:00 P.M. "I pick up the first one," she says, "and it has no job objective on it. I have no idea what this person wants or where he would fit in my organization. It goes in the reject pile. What you're saying by *not* putting an objective on your résumé is, 'Here, Ms. Employment Manager, *you* decide where I should work.' Would you go to a car dealer and say, 'You decide which car I should buy'?"

What should you put in a job objective? "You can be very specific," says Mathews. "If you know what you want, say so. If you only know the general area, be a little less specific; but tell the employment manager *something.*"

You cannot write a job objective if you haven't done your homework; because, ideally, you are really rephrasing the job description. Federated's description included: ability to work with and supervise administrative personnel, process work flow, establish office procedures, interact with management, and provide daily office management.

Karen tailored her objective to those exact requirements. She also included the kind of organization she wished to work for and how Federated Finance would benefit from hiring her. Here is her objective:

A position as Office Manager with a growth-oriented organization that will benefit from my

---

Excerpts from a Functional Résumé

Objective

A position as Office Manager . . .

Areas of Strength

Managing People	Have had experience in all aspects of office management, from annual goal planning . . .
	Supervised administrative and data processing support staff . . .
Developing Systems	Develop systems; organize and codify information accurately . . .
	Set up monthly inventory system for ACME promotional materials and stationery; coordinated office communications system with six branch offices . . .
Problem Solving	Bring innovation and creativity to problem solving . . .
	Constructively helped staff unravel mistakes and improve operations procedures . . .

"Professional Experience" encompasses all the jobs you've held. In a chronological résumé, you would list each job, in reverse chronological order, beginning with the most recent, just as you did on your lists. You may choose to divide your jobs into career-related and non-career-related, or leave out the ones that don't seem to relate to your objective. In a chronological

résumé, that, of course, will leave some discernible gaps in your work history.

In this category, be sure you convey both qualifications and accomplishments, no matter how you organize that information.

"Educational Experience" is the next common heading. Here you must decide whether the school you attended or the degree you received is the most important point to list first. Honors and awards can be included under "Education" or may be listed under a separate category, depending on where they would have the most impact. You will have to use your own judgment about mentioning such information as major and minor subjects, grade point averages, test scores, standing in your class, courses you've taken, and the high school you attended—depending on their direct relationship to your job objective and the requirements of the job.

"Extracurricular Activities" include groups in which you've been an active member or an officer, volunteer work of all kinds, activities you put on your *Things I Love to Do* list, and anything else for which you have not been paid. Don't just list group or organization names; list accomplishments. What did you do for that group? What contribution did you make? The rule, as always, is to check your entries against your goal. Does this have anything to do with your target job, your objective, the qualifications you're supporting with tangible evidence that you truly are qualified? If not, don't list it!

Activities can be subdivided into types: "Writing Activities," "Athletic Activities," "Political Activities." This is one example of how you can individualize your headings, of which you've only seen a small sampling. Others you may wish to use are: "Publications," "Military Service," "Travel," "Languages Spoken and Written," "Athletic Experience," "Personal Data," "Political Background," "Honors and Awards," "Licenses and Certificates," "Interests" (things you love to do), and on and on, almost without end. The list is as long and as varied as your creativity can make it.

What Should You Leave Out?

Résumés are intended to be read, and each of them competes with hundreds of others for that honor. Put yourself in Pat Mathews' place for a moment. There you are, sitting in your living room at 11:00 at night, staring bleary-eyed at a pile of 200 résumés you must scan before you can collapse for the night. You pick one up. You put it down immediately—in the reject pile. Why? What turned you off so quickly?

A long list of possible résumé turnoffs could be compiled. Here I'll mention some of the most glaring and common no-nos:

- *Wordiness and repetition.* Make your résumé as concise as possible. Edit it several times deleting any words that aren't essential.
- *Erasures, cross-outs, handwritten corrections.* Your résumé should be neatly and accurately typed. If it isn't, retype it, or have someone do it for you, if your typing is as bad as mine is.
- *Onionskin or erasable paper.* They may look nice, but these make a résumé hard to read and prone to smudging.
- *Faint and/or broken type.* Always use a fresh typewriter ribbon for dark, clear print.
- *Photographs.* Do not include a photo. Your personal appearance will be considered when you make it to the interview.
- *Birth date, health data, marital and family status.* Leave out all personal information that may seem irrelevant to the reader or that will reveal more than you should.
- *References.* Most employers will ask for these and check them, but that happens later, if and when a job offer is imminent.

The rest is almost too obvious to mention, but sometimes the obvious goes unnoticed. Do not include your references—verified or unchecked, appropriate or inappropriate. Use references targeted to the position and send them later or include them separately. Don't put them in your résumé. Do not skimp on information, so the employer is left wondering what you really did accomplish or where you've spent the last ten years. On the other hand, don't tell your life story. A multipage résumé with everything you ever wanted to know but were afraid to ask will put the employment manager to sleep.

Finally, avoid generalizations, exaggerations, gimmicks, clichés, disorganization, and—need I say it?—outright lies. If an employer ever finds out you fabricated your information, you, not your résumé, will be on the reject pile.

Now that you know what you're going to say, we'll move along, in Chapter 6, to how you'll want to say it.

Chapter 6

Creating a Class Act

You've already seen that your message will never get a hearing (or a reading) if there are red flags all over it that shout, *"Don't read this!"* We covered a few of those red flags in the last chapter. In this one, you're going to explore two important components of style and form: how your message should be verbally and graphically conveyed. In other words, how should you say it, and how should you package what you say? (In the Appendix, you can see several representative examples of the various sorts of résumés prepared by people in different circumstances, starting with the one Karen Kincaid sent to Federated Finance.)

What Should It Look Like?

We're going to begin with the packaging, rather than what's in the package, because that is the very first thing an employment manager sees. If your résumé's appearance turns him or her off, out it goes.

On the other hand, if your résumé makes a positive impression and stands out from the crowd based on its appearance alone, you've just scored a point over the competition.

The basics. Obviously, your offering should be clean and neat and easy to read. It should be well organized, with headings separating clean blocks of words, either in paragraph form or with each entry preceded by a bullet to draw your attention to what it says.

It should also be consistent—in its presentation both of information and of you, the person it represents. If you present one category in paragraph form, don't shift your style to bullets in the next. Decide on a "look" and stick with it.

Typed or typeset? This brings us to the question of typing or typesetting and how you decide between them. Personnel professionals are not wildly enthusiastic about typeset résumés. For one thing, they know a typeset résumé wasn't created for a single purpose or a specific job. You must have at least 100 of them, to justify the expense, especially if you've had them printed, as well.

"If a résumé is written clearly and honestly and is structured so that it highlights the person's strengths, I see no reason for it to be typeset or done with super snazz, unless that person is applying for an image-making position," says Ramona Howard. Her view reflects the opinion of most people who read résumés, though Pat Mathews feels that typesetting can be the "icing on the cake" if it supports visually what you've said in the copy or demonstrates how well you use the tools of your trade. If such factors as design, paper, color, or type are part of the message you wish to convey, suggests Mathews, they're appropriate.

One word of caution: If you do decide to go the extra mile with your graphics, you'd better know what you're doing or get help from someone who does. There is nothing worse than a designed, typeset, and printed résumé that is poorly done. When that one makes an impression, it's an indelible one.

There is one other way to convey your message in type, and that is with a word processor or computer with word processing software. What's wrong with that? Nothing, especially if you have access to a letter-quality printer. Dot matrix is generally unacceptable, but if the output looks as if it had been typed on a good typewriter—and with most printers, it will look even better than the best typewriter—it's fine.

One obvious advantage of using a word processor is the ability to store information for later use or rearrange it to suit a different purpose. If you follow the advice to create a series of résumés rather than one, or to target very precisely every job you want, word processing will save you hours of time and will produce a perfectly correct résumé every time.

One page or two? One of the first questions new résumé writers ask, in terms of form, is, "Shouldn't it all be on one page?" If you learned to write a résumé in school, you are probably a slave to this idea; but it may work against you if you've added significantly to your experience since you graduated. "There's nothing wrong with a two-page résumé," insists Pat Mathews. "Ten years after college, if you're still cramming everything onto a single page, you're probably leaving out some important information."

Paper and color. First, the paper. It should be at least 20-pound bond, and it should feel right to the person holding it. Remember, the first thing an employment manager does is pick up your résumé; the second is look at it. If it feels cheap or thin or sleazy, it has already conveyed a negative impression of you. Choose a paper that is 100 percent cotton fiber, for a weight and feel that makes a silent statement of their own on your behalf.

Second, color. Need I say, nothing bright, garish, outlandish, or pastel? White is safe, and white comes in 57 varieties, believe it or not. Off-white is acceptable, as are light beige, eggshell (more yellow than off-white), and pale gray. Everything else must be viewed as suspect and used with great discretion, if at all.

How Do You Say It?

Putting your best foot forward. If you're using the chronological format, you will lead with your strongest suit. If your educational background is the most impressive thing you have to offer in terms of the employer's needs, your first heading will be "Education." If, on the other hand, your education is irrelevant or sparse, you will bury it. If you didn't finish college, or your degree is in elementary education or industrial engineering and you're seeking a job in marketing management, your education will not shout, "See how well I fit the bill."

Even if your educational background is not what you'd like it to be, you may have gained all of your relevant experience on the job. Obviously, your best credentials are in your professional experience.

Under every heading, such as "Professional Experience," you will have a number of listings. Each will represent a job you've held. When you describe the job, you'll have to make a judgment call regarding what is most important—your title or the company name. Whatever you decide, all of the entries must be formatted consistently.

Are you a doer? Show it! There are two ways to write your entries: in sentence or modified-sentence form, or in phrases or listings. Sentences and modified sentences have verbs in them; phrases or listings do not. For most things you will write, verbs pack a punch. They're active; they show that you've done something. And that's half of what an accomplishment is supposed to do; the rest is to tell what you did. Look at a few of Karen's listed accomplishments:

Supervised administrative personnel
Established office procedures and systems
Set up monthly inventory system
Developed training track for staff

Every one of Karen's qualifications and accomplishments begins with an action verb. When Federated's vice-president reads them, he will form an impression of a person who acts and does. Employers are looking for doers. That's hardly a news flash.

Numbers are powerful tools. If your accomplishments involve sales successes, how much did you sell? If you managed or trained a lot of people, how many? When you are tooting your horn about results or achievements, if a number fits, use it.

It should go without saying, but . . . Spell it correctly. If you don't know, look it up. Punctuate it correctly. Same rule. Type it correctly. If you can't proofread your own work, and few people can, ask a friend. Be consistent. This applies to everything—style, format, sentence structure, types of headings, what's under the headings, capitalization, punctuation—*everything.*

Is This All There Is?

What else could there possibly be left to do, you ask? The rest of the package, of course; and it includes your cover letter, written on paper that matches your résumé and inserted in an envelope that matches both, along with—if you went the typeset and printed route— a business card.

What goes in the cover letter? Marvin McMillian sums up his advice in three short sentences: "Keep your résumé simple. Stress relevant experience. And concentrate on your cover letter." Dr. McMillian pays attention to cover letters. "Chances are the person wrote it himself," he says. "It's not structured like a résumé, it involves more self-expression, and it may say something intriguing. If you're applying for a marketing job, there ought to be something in your letter that indicates you can market yourself."

Pat Mathews takes an opposing view. Speaking as someone who works for a very large corporation, she observes: "Employment managers rarely read a cover letter. I give them a 30-second scan to see what words jump out."

The prevailing view, however, is that the cover letter says a great deal about you and can pack a punch, especially if you know how to write a powerful benefit statement. Benefit statements are part of the language of salespeople who sell to the needs of their customers. A benefit statement consists of three parts: a statement of the customer's need, a description of a feature of what you're selling, and a way of linking those two things together. In Karen's cover letter, she used the following benefit statement:

Knowing your need for a person who is able to provide guidance, support, and direction to administrative personnel, I believe my extensive background in managing and motivating a staff of 19, creating and implementing office procedures and systems, and serving as a personnel administrator in my present position would save you valuable transition time, since I would be able to function as Office Manager immediately.

Coordinating the pieces. Your packaging must be as consistent as everything inside. That means the paper on which you print your résumé and your letterhead should be the same. And they should, of course, match the envelope you put them in. Whether they are typed or typeset, they should be set up identically. If your name and address are centered a half-inch from the top of the page on one sheet, they should be in exactly the same place on the other. Naturally, you should use the same typewriter, printer, or type style.

If you do typeset and print your résumé, you might consider printing 100 sheets of letterhead and then overprinting your résumé on 25 to 50 of those sheets. When you buy your own paper, it usually comes in boxes of 500, as do the envelopes; so you'll have plenty of second sheets for letters or leftover paper should you wish to revise at a later time. Private "business cards" only make sense if you do typeset and print, since they add a touch of class and don't cost very much to do.

What is all this going to cost? The big-ticket items are typesetting and printing, and even those costs can vary quite a bit. If you go first class, typesetting and production (arranging the type on boards as camera-ready art for the printer) can run to $150 or more.

Printing costs will depend on the caliber of printer

you use and such variables as number of pieces to print (letterhead, one- or two-page résumé, envelopes, cards) and the colors you choose. If you are printing in black ink on paper you've already purchased, a quick-print operation may charge as little as $13. Odd colors or two-color projects will obviously cost more.

Typing is certainly inexpensive. So is using a word processor or computer, if you have one. Duplicating by using a high-quality copier is perfectly acceptable. The important thing is to have a clean original. You can even use colored paper in most copiers, and some do print in two colors.

If you decided that you have no graphic sense at all and want a professional designer or résumé service to arrange elements on the page for you, you will have to take their fees into account. The same is true if you have your résumé written by a professional writer or a service.

Obviously, costs vary with the amount and quality of service you purchase. A good designer will charge either by the hour or by the project. A first-class type-setter or production house can be very expensive.

As always, you will get what you pay for; but you may not have to pay for very much at all and still produce a dynamite-looking, highly effective résumé. Paper, by the way, will be the least expensive item on your list: You can buy a box of 100 percent cotton fiber paper at a good paper warehouse for as little as $16.

Conclusion

Getting That Act Together

Remember what a résumé is designed to do? To create an image of you in the employer's mind and to get you an interview. But it won't do that sitting on your desk. It is not the purpose of this little book to give you a crash course in job hunting as well as in résumé writing, but a few words are certainly in order about how you begin that process.

Where do you start? I asked that question when you began the résumé process, and it's surely the one you're asking now. Well, you've already started.

You know what you want and how to look for it. You can even create your ideal job in your mind and write a description of it. In fact, you have. Assuming that you aren't holding such an ad in your hand right now, you certainly know how and where to look for one.

The national publications (such as daily issues of the *Wall Street Journal* or less frequent editions of *Business Week*) and major city newspapers (like the *New York Times,* the *Washington Post,* and others) are wonderful sources if you're considering relocating anywhere in the United States. If you don't plan to leave your home base, however, you will probably want to concentrate on your local publications for jobs in your immediate area.

The other invaluable and uncommon skill you have developed is knowing how to network successfully. You're also an old hand at interviewing by now.

Perhaps you have now conquered your fear—or most of it—of calling a total stranger and requesting an appointment. Maybe you have improved the way you handle yourself in those interviews after doing only a few of them. You're going to thank yourself for getting over that hurdle when you begin your job interviewing. The poise and confidence you now have will take you a long way when you talk to potential employers.

So you have several new skills, all of which combine to launch you into the job-hunting process. There are many other sources of job leads, of course, in addition to want ads and networking, though these two have the advantage of pointing you toward real, existing jobs. You might also consider job-placement departments at local colleges and universities, even if you are not a student; employment agencies that specialize in your field; placement services of professional organizations that relate to your career goals (you may have to join those organizations in order to use their placement services); professional career counselors; or poring through lists of major employers in your community and choosing the ones appropriate to your skills and interests (you can find such lists at your local chamber of commerce).

Remember Your Marketing Mind-set

Finding good sources and resources is only half the task; the other half is maintaining the mentality of a marketer. What you're looking for are the needs in the marketplace that *you* can fill better than anyone else. Then you have to prove that to the person with the needs.

That was exactly the challenge Karen faced when she finished her résumé—on time. She was almost breathless when she finally hand-delivered it to her friend Ellen, over lunch. "Now what?" she asked. "What do I do next?" Ellen explained that résumés had been pouring in ever since the ad appeared the previous Sunday. "Either this must be a fantastic job, or there are a lot of people out of work," she told Karen, whose heart sank at the news.

Karen was sure she didn't have a chance. But she was wrong. The vice-president called her the next day. Her letter and résumé had piqued his interest, and Ellen had spoken highly of her, he said. Could she meet with him on Saturday morning? Could she! She'd be there with bells on.

The Interview

The vice-president had a name. It was Jim Roberts. "Call me Jim," he said warmly, and picked up Karen's résumé. He liked it, he told her. It showed a lot of effort, and it told him she had done her homework. "I certainly know what you've done and how that all applies to Federated," Jim said. "And there's no question that it *does* apply."

The interview lasted 2½ hours, but it never seemed like an interview to Karen. Jim was very nice. He certainly knew his business, and he asked her a hundred questions about office systems and word processing software, how she handled disputes between employees, what she usually did about staff meetings, what she felt was the best way to motivate a difficult employee, how she handled someone who was yelling at her or crying, and more.

It wasn't the questions that surprised Karen; it was her own answers—solid and sound and sure. Jim was interested in what she had to say. When she answered one of his questions, he listened and nodded and commented. He seemed to feel she knew what she was talking about. "Well, I do!" Karen thought to herself. "I really do."

He shook her hand at the door and asked again about her references. "Yes, it's fine to call them all," she assured him. He didn't call them all—only two, and one was Karen's manager. "I would hate to lose her," he told Jim at the end of their long phone conversation. "She's my right arm, and I don't know how I'll replace her."

The End of the Story

The following week, Karen returned for her "second interview," this one with the two managing partners. She had no idea how they would react to her or what their input on the hiring decision might be. She felt she was ready for just about anything, but what happened was not what she had expected.

She walked into Jim's office, expecting to meet the partners. Instead, he said: "Let's get right down to business. I've given this a lot of thought; and if you want this job, it's yours."

Karen is now the office manager at Federated Finance Company. A respected member of the management team, she began her new job with an $11,000 increase in salary.

Karen is not a fictitious character, and her story, except for a detail or two, is true. She went through every single step outlined in this book and tailored her résumé to a real job description. She did get the job, after only one real interview. But even she does not believe that her résumé alone got her the job. That wasn't its purpose, nor its result.

There are *many* elements involved in finding and being offered the right job. One is assuredly the hard work that goes into researching and writing the best, most clearly targeted résumé possible. Another is taking the image your résumé has conveyed of you and bringing it to life by the way you look and speak and dress and present yourself when you meet the potential employer in person. Still another is preparing for and successfully negotiating the interview once you are there. Perhaps we might even say that luck is a factor in connecting with the right job.

Karen had the good fortune to hear of a job opening from a friend. The rest was up to her, as it will be up to you when you begin your own personal job search. Your résumé will be an important piece of that search. If you've used this guide as a workbook, going through each of the steps along the way, you already have your résumé in hand and are ready for the next step in this adventure. Good luck!

Appendix—Sample Résumés

On the following pages are several sample résumés. They represent people in different stages of their lives, seeking different jobs in different ways. The author has included three résumés created and used by her two daughters as examples of three of the four categories mentioned in this book.

1. Karen Kincaid's combination résumé, of which you've seen pieces along the way, concentrates on objective/qualifications/accomplishments, all geared to a specific job description. It led to the interview, which, in turn, led to the job offer.

2. Leslie was still in college when she wrote this chronological résumé, geared to a position in restaurant management. As part of her overall strategy, it helped to get her several interviews within a short period of time. She was offered the management-training position she wanted within two weeks of her graduation.
3. Terry has a functional résumé, highlighting her experiences in marketing and sales, as well as in teaching and counseling—two very different areas. Her objective should have been more targeted, so that a potential employer would have known exactly what kind of a position she was seeking.
4. In her second attempt, a bold promotional résumé, Terry spelled out her objective and her qualifications for a sales position in the sporting equipment or apparel industry. She used a professional artist to design both a personal logo and a format for her presentation.

KAREN KINCAID
321 Springhaven Street
Maryville, Mo. 63105
(214) 555-2424

OBJECTIVE

A position as Office Manager with a growth-oriented organization that will benefit from my skills and experience in communicating with and motivating a broad range of people and my demonstrated organizational ability.

QUALIFICATIONS

— Have had experience in all aspects of office management, from annual goal planning to day-to-day troubleshooting.
— Manage people well by encouraging a free flow of ideas with staff, delegating responsibility, and motivating for greater productivity.
— Communicate by listening attentively and presenting ideas clearly.
— Work well with all levels of people, including clients, upper management, peers, and staff.
— Develop systems; organize and codify information accurately; maintain and update records regularly.
— Bring innovation and creativity to problem solving.
— Juggle many tasks simultaneously, often meeting tight deadlines; work well under pressure.
— Take criticism and feedback well, following through on suggestions.

ACCOMPLISHMENTS

— Supervised administrative and data processing support staff.
— Established office procedures and systems for that staff.
— Coordinated corporate office communications system with six branch offices around the United States.

- Set up monthly inventory system for ACME's promotional materials, stationery, and supplies.
- Developed training track for administrative staff members and conducted the training of new and experienced staff members.
- Coordinated and planned participation in national and regional trade shows.
- Coordinated psychological test administration and evaluations.
- Coached and counseled staff to maximize productivity of administrative personnel.
- Helped staff unravel mistakes and improve operations procedures.

EMPLOYMENT HISTORY

ACME Corporation
Maryville, Mo.

1985–present	Supervisor, Marketing Administration and Data Processing
1984–1985	Administrative Assistant, Marketing Department
1983–1984	Administrative Assistant, Operations
1979–1983	Administrative Assistant, Sales Department
1976–1979	Receptionist/Clerk-Typist, Sales Department
1974–1976	Typist, Sales Department

EDUCATION

1973–1974	Maryville Community College; Maryville, Mo.
1984	Three-day seminar in supervisory skills for new managers
1982	Night class in customer-relations/telephone skills
1979	Night class in public speaking
1978	Night class in speed typing
1976	Night class in shorthand

Leslie A. LinKemer

20414 THOMPSON DRIVE CHESTERFIELD, MO 60605 (314) 555-3030

PROFESSIONAL OBJECTIVE

Seeking a position in a high caliber food service or lodging organization that will enable me to make use of my experience and education in this field, gain additional on-the-job experience, and meet the qualifications for a management job.

EDUCATION

University of Missouri—Columbia; Columbia, Missouri
August, 1980—present
> B.S. degree, August, 1984.
> Major: Food Service and Lodging Management, School of Agriculture.

PROFESSIONAL EXPERIENCE

The Original Bobby Buford, Columbia, Missouri
August, 1982—present
> Hostess and Cocktail Waitress.

Bristol Bar and Grill, St. Louis, Missouri
May, 1983—August, 1983
> Food Waitress.

Godfather's Ristorante, St. Louis, Missouri
May, 1981—August, 1982
> (part-time, summers, and vacations) Cashier and Hostess.

Leslie A. LinKemer

20414 THOMPSON DRIVE   CHESTERFIELD, MO 60605   (314) 555-3030

Caleco's, St. Louis, Missouri
March, 1979—August, 1980
 Busperson, Hostess, and Carry-out Waitress.

PERSONAL AND PROFESSIONAL ASSETS

As a professional in the food service and lodging industry, I relate well to customers and fellow workers; learn new systems easily and rapidly; take direction well; and have experience in a wide variety of food service establishments. Personally, I am dependable, enthusiastic, conscientious, eager to learn, honest, and committed to my employer.

AFFILIATIONS & ACTIVITIES

Alpha Gamma Delta Sorority, UMC, Columbia, Missouri: Active Member.

Distributive Education Clubs of America (DECA), Parkway Central Senior High,
 St. Louis, Missouri: Secretary.

PERSONAL DATA

Birthdate: June 22, 1962
Health: Excellent
References: Available upon request
Flexibility: Willing to travel or relocate

TERRY LYNN LINKEMER
20414 Thompson Drive
Chesterfield, MO 60605
Home phone (314) 555-3030

PROFESSIONAL OBJECTIVE

Seeking a position that will take full advantage of my background in sales, teaching, and interpersonal skills, as well as offer me the opportunity for increasing levels of responsibility and professional growth.

MARKETING & SALES EXPERIENCE

Overview: Have worked in a variety of businesses—retail sporting goods, travel, athletic clubs, pharmacies, restaurants—selling products ranging from adventure tours and athletic equipment to food and liquor.

Accomplishments: Dealt with a variety of clientele; uncovered customer needs and meshed employer's products with those needs; worked productively with outside vendors, travel agents, representatives of the transportation and hotel/resort industries, and the general public.

Employers: International Athletic Club, Denver, Colorado; Range Tours, Denver; Sport Stalker, Inc., Keystone, Colorado; John Gardner Tennis Ranch, Keystone; Esteban's Restaurant, Keystone; The Ranch House, Columbia, Missouri; Omni Sports, St. Louis, Missouri; Forum Center Pharmacy, St. Louis.

TEACHING AND COUNSELING EXPERIENCE

Overview: Worked with people of all ages in teaching, counseling, and administrative capacities in both professional and volunteer positions.

Accomplishments: Completed a three-year staff training program at a co-ed camp; taught swimming and water skiing; studied sign language for the deaf and utilized that training in teaching swimming and other skills to the hearing impaired; assisted in teaching self defense classes for both men and women;

completed Level-I certification for Project Stream (ropes course training) and worked with local boyscout troups; researched and ordered materials related to Missouri hiking and waterways; lifeguarded, taught swimming, and assisted in pool management for large athletic facility.

Employers and Sponsors: Jewish Community Centers Association (JCCA), St. Louis, Missouri; Camp Sabra, Rocky Mount, Missouri; University Pool, University of Missouri-Columbia (UMC), Columbia, Missouri; Physical Education Department, UMC, Columbia, Missouri; Webster College, St. Louis; Taum Sauk Wilderness, Inc., Columbia; Missouri School for the Deaf, Fulton, Missouri.

PERSONAL AND PROFESSIONAL ASSETS

I offer a potential employer a high level of energy and enthusiasm, experience with a wide variety of people, background in sales, interpersonal skills, a sense of commitment to my employer, and the ability to discern and respond to the needs of customers or clients. My education and first-hand experience have honed my skills and prepared me to make a significant contribution to any organizations. I would, of course, be eager to complete any additional training required for the position.

EDUCATIONAL EXPERIENCE

Bachelor of Educational Studies—University of Missouri—Columbia, College of Education, December, 1982. Major in Sport/Business and Outdoor Education.

Additional Training: Private Pilot Ground School, Parkway Central Senior High School, St. Louis, Missouri; Fundamentals of Black & White Photography, UMC, Columbia, Missouri; Sign language for the deaf, UMC, Columbia, Missouri; Missouri School for the Deaf, Fulton, Missouri; Fundamental Sales Skills, Wilson Learning Corporation, Columbia, Missouri, 1982; Dimensional Sales Training, Psychological Associates, Inc., St. Louis, Missouri, January, 1984.

Conventional resumes represent conventional people. If you choose to read on, you'll discover you're dealing with neither of those. Conventional preparation for employment involves packaging the skills and education one has to match whatever jobs happen to exist.

That was never my intent. My planned and executed objective was to prepare for **one** job — selling a quality line of products for a quality name in the sports equipment or apparel industry. I have prepared to do this by personal participation in all levels of sports competition; by formal education; and by active, practical working experience in the sports/recreation business.

The detail that follows will, hopefully, demonstrate that my preparation was parallel to what you would have suggested I accomplish to fit the needs of your organization, had we talked 15 years ago.

PERSONAL PARTICIPATION

I am an athlete — not a fitness faddist or a weekend jock — but a person committed to the athletic life. I am at home on a tennis or racquetball court, the ski slopes, running or biking trails, in or on the water. My involvement with sports includes both participation and teaching. At Camp Sabra in Rocky Mount, Missouri, in addition to completing a three-year staff training program, I taught swimming and water skiing. Then, I studied sign language for the deaf and used that training to teach swimming and other athletic skills to the hearing impaired; taught self defense classes for both men and women at the University of Missouri–Columbia; and attained level-I certification in Project Stream (ropes course training) and worked with Boy Scout troops.

ACADEMIC BACKGROUND

My B.E.S. degree from the University of Missouri–Columbia is in two areas: **Sport Business** and **Outdoor Education.** In the first, I gained a broad-based understanding of the complexities of selling the concept of physical fitness and its accouterments to the public. Outdoor Education focused on teaching a wide array of skills, using the outdoors as a classroom. Together, this course of study prepared me to present an awareness of a skill or sport, sell its equipment and apparel, and actually teach the skills necessary to use those products.

That undergraduate schooling has been enhanced by participation in two sales training programs: **Fundamental Sales Skills,** Wilson Learning Corporation, 1982; and **Dimensional Sales Training,** Psychological Associates, Inc., 1984.

Terry
Lynn
Linkemer

20414 THOMPSON DR., CHESTERFIELD, MO 60605 • (314) 555-3030

PROFESSIONAL EXPERIENCE

Beyond the formal education and auxiliary courses, I have found my on-the-job training in retail sports to be of incomparable value. I am a salesperson. The products and services I have sold have been consistently associated with sports. My experience in direct retail sales has been with highly respected organizations, including: **Omni Sports** in St. Louis, a full-line sporting goods equipment and apparel store . . . **Sports Stalker, Inc.,** at the base of Keystone Mountain in Colorado, a specialty ski shop handling the finest in hard and soft goods . . . **John Gardner Tennis Ranch,** also in Keystone, a high caliber tennis facility and school, with a pro shop selling top of the line tennis gear and accessories . . . and the **Alpine Shop,** a mountaineering store, specializing in down-hill and cross-country ski-related equipment and apparel in the winter and camping, backpacking, rock climbing, and other related wilderness activities in the summer.

Selling adventure getaways and vacations for **Range Tours** in Denver and a myriad of specialized part-time positions at the **Jewish Community Centers Association** in St. Louis have helped me to complement and augment my direct sales background by honing my people skills and increasing my levels of responsibility.

PERSONAL DATA & ASSETS

I was born October 27, 1959, in Champaign, Illinois, and am in superb health. I would be happy to furnish references and will eagerly travel or relocate to meet the demands of the position. I bring to all professional endeavors a high level of energy and enthusiasm. I offer well-developed interpersonal skills, a strong sense of commitment to the task and my employer, and the flexibility only experience with a wide range of people can generate. I will be happy to complete any additional training required for the job.

Terry
Lynn
Linkemer

20414 THOMPSON DR., CHESTERFIELD, MO 60605 · (314) 555-3030

ABOUT THE AUTHOR

Bobbi Linkemer has been a journalist and communicator for 20 years. Her first article, a humor piece chronicling the woes of a handball widow, was published in a national handball magazine and used as a basis for an article on the fast-growing sport in the *Chicago Tribune* Sunday magazine section.

After several years of free-lancing, Ms. Linkemer was named editor of *The St. Louisan,* a general-interest city magazine. Her love affair with magazine journalism continued, taking her to a business-oriented publication entitled *St. Louis Commerce.* After seven years of full-time magazine work, she made the leap from media to corporate communications, heading up employee publications for an international, *Fortune* 500 company and a major midwestern bank-holding company.

Her full-time professional experience since then has included creating and producing a number of publications for various audiences, including public and media relations, advertising, marketing, management, and direct sales. In the meantime, she has continued to free-lance on the local and national levels, teach a series of writers' workshops, and act as a consultant and writer of corporate marketing materials.

She is presently Marketing Manager for Psychological Associates, Inc., an internationally recognized training and development firm.